AF284171

Gianni, Jan & Marcello Liscia

WORKBOOK
DEDICATION

Dedication to the work at hand, with heart and soul,
24 hours a day

Illustrations:
Herman Reichold

Dedication is the first of five books in the D.R.E.A.M. of LEADERS®
publication series.

1ˢᵗ edition 2018

Imprint
© 2018 Gianni, Jan & Marcello Liscia

Layout, cover + worksheets: Franziska Eikel, Liscia Consulting
English translation by Ramey Rieger: doitwritetranslations@gmx.de

Text + Layout:
Biographiewerkstatt Böddeker
Ellerstraße 26 – 33100 Paderborn
Telephone: 05293 - 9327816

Print and publishers: : Books on Demand, Norderstedt
ISBN: 978-3-7528-5787-0

Table of Contents

"Quality emerges from the love for detail."[1]
Andreas Tenzer (German philosopher and educator)

Dear Reader,

We are delighted that you have chosen our *Workbook: Dedication*! Apparently, you enjoyed our book *D.R.E.A.M. of LEADERS® Leadership is not an Illusion* and are inspired to intensify and solidify your insights. Of course, that pleases us no end! As a rule, we work with our clients over a longer period, developing a personal relationship. Now, this workbook offers us the opportunity to work closely with you, so you may encounter personal subjects, questions and tasks. This is what we do.

Or maybe this book fell into your hands purely incidentally, and now you're wondering what this D.R.E.A.M. of LEADERS® could be? Then let us fill you in on the basics.

For over 15 years, we have been guiding and promoting people's professional development. For us, there is no greater honor. Thus, we have made cultivating leaders our primary responsibility, most specifically, by developing the D.R.E.A.M. Formula[2]:

D Dedication: Wholehearted commitment to mission, 24 hours a day
R Responsibility: Assuming full responsibility for your decisions, for your staff and for yourself
E Education: Ensuring you and your staff evolve
A Attitude: Living and communicating your personal mindset (philosophy) and values
M Motivation: Commitment as the foundation of all deeds

---

[1] Unspecified quotes are taken from *Book of Quotations* (Bassermann-Verlag, 2013) or from digital quote collections.

[2] D.R.E.A.M.-Formel® is a protected trademark owned by Liscia Consulting and registered with the German Patent and Trademark Office.

The D.R.E.A.M. Formula acronym can also be understood as a checklist, illustrating the self-concept of a leader. It is how leadership can be understood and lived. However, since this a very complex, multi-facetted topic, our first publication, *D.R.E.A.M. of LEADERS® Leadership is not an Illusion*, could only convey an initial Impression of what we understand leadership to be.

In the meantime, we have created a workbook on each letter of the D.R.E.A.M. Formula® expanding on certain aspects, providing more examples and with worksheets at the end of each chapter for a practical application of acquired knowledge. The workbooks are intentionally conceived to be read and used independently of the first book. The basic structure of each chapter has been preserved and complemented by additional examples. Thus, insights from the other books is not a prerequisite.

This workbook addresses the topic *Dedication*. We will shed light on employee and employer engagement, go into the difference between manager and leader, introduce the D.R.E.A.M.-Score®, a method we developed to measure leadership quality, as well as speak about future visions and leadership strategy.[1]

Enjoy reading and learning about how to practice your Dedication!

---

[1] To enhance readability, we have alternated masculine and feminine non-specific personal pronouns per chapter. Hence, in this context, we consider both genders gender-neutral and hope they are understood as such.

Dedication

CEO:	He just doesn't identify with us, with our company!
LISCIA:	He doesn't?
CEO:	No, he doesn't. He fulfills his contract to the letter, but that's it!
LISCIA:	What do *you* give *him* that's not in the contract?
CEO:	Pardon?
LISCIA:	When was the last time you surprised *him*, or any other employee for that matter? Pleasantly surprised.
CEO:	Hmm.

"Yes, I do!"

What is the stuff of executive dreams? Business leaders dream of hard-hitting teams, of powerful teams, of dedicated employees. In today's working world, teams are often fragmented. Team members are scattered over the five continents, throughout various countries, embodying various cultures, speaking various languages. This is the reality of global leadership.

The question, then, for a managing director is, "How can I successfully lead my team under these circumstances?" An essential prerequisite for a company's growth and impact is employee engagement. Dedicated employees don't stand around waiting for instructions. They share the thought process, act independently, assume responsibility for the health and well-being of the entire enterprise. They are not only exceptionally good at their jobs, they also nurture teamwork and the work environment.

Yet, not all employees are equally committed. Within a team or department, you will find highly dedicated employees working side by side with colleagues who may fulfill their responsibilities, but only that, and no more.

According to a 2017 Gallup poll, Germany suffers a decided lack of committed employees – a mere 15 percent, while 15 percent of employees are actively disengaged.[1] How does an actively disengaged employee behave? He seizes every opportunity to ruin you and your business.

Later in this chapter, we will talk about Georg, an actively disengaged branch manager who fully intentionally sabotaged his company, incurring

---

[1] Cf. Gallup Inc., *State of the Global Workplace*, 2017

massive damage. To eliminate sabotage from the start, we approach employee engagement as a nuptial agreement. No different than in a personal context, where two people promise themselves to one another, saying "Yes, I do!" You, the boss or superior, expect your future employee to enter an emotional relationship with you. You expect him to declare, "Yes! I love this company and will remain until the end of my professional life do us part."

When taking this approach to employee engagement – as an emotional commitment on both sides – then it should be directly reflected in the job description. For example, "Dear Prospective Employee, we expect you to love this company; to dedicate yourself to this company; to love your job and our customers, as we love you. We want an emotionally binding relationship. Only then, will we accept you."

Practically applied, the manager could say to the prospective staff member, "I expect more. I expect you to work 10, 12 or 14 hours a day. I expect you to be underway five days a week, in five different countries. I expect you to burn the midnight oil, polishing your presentation until two in the morning, perfecting it for the meeting the next day." Only a prospective employee acknowledging and (gladly) accepting these expectations should be allowed to enter the engagement and sign the employment contract. This emotional connection is the seed that grows into a team or company. Only emotionally bonded co-workers can be brand ambassadors for your business. They express themselves with convincing positivity when talking about their employer. They earnestly represent your company and its products. They automatically strive to be better; reach for more. It is very much worth the effort. Dedicated staff members are more productive, contributing to your company's growth, while radically reducing work accidents, staff turnover and absenteeism.

Now, with this in mind, imagine three employees of a globally active enterprise. After a strenuous day at the trade fair, the trio decides to have a beer together in the hotel bar before turning in for the night. While sipping their drinks, they overhear a married couple speaking disparagingly about the company which employs the three colleagues. The employees' reactions couldn't have been more disparate, and clearly illustrates each one's degree of engagement.

The actively engaged colleague doesn't hesitate to join the conversation, defending his company passionately. He is a prime example of a brand ambassador. The moment the disengaged employee grasps what they're talking about, he grabs his jacket and leaves the bar, not wanting to have anything to do with the discussion. His actively disengaged colleague, however, also joins the conversation, but not to defend his workplace. He wholeheartedly agrees with the couple's negative opinion, providing them with further proof of the company's failings, confirming it is indeed, 'the pits.'

Many examples of internal sabotage, in both word and deed, have made the press over the past few years. Several mailmen were brought to court for deliberately refusing to deliver the mail, simply throwing their letter-bags in the garbage. The same was true of parcel service providers. The number of customer complaints rose dramatically – packages arrived opened, contents were either missing or damaged. If a recipient wasn't at home, carriers simply threw the parcel over the garden fence and signed the receipt of delivery themselves, or they left a failed delivery notice without bothering to ring the bell at all. In some cases, not even a notice was given, or the handwriting was illegible.[1] Such employees thoroughly enjoy the consequences of their actions, knowing full well they are ruining their employer's reputation, causing slews of customers to take their business elsewhere.

Another revolting example of active employee disengagement was related to us by a client, the CEO of a Northern Germany food chain. One of his branch managers, the aforementioned Georg, deliberately ignored the cockroaches and mice overrunning his store. He couldn't have cared less about the health risk the vermin posed to his co-workers and customers – he certainly didn't shop there or eat in the store's bistro.

Eventually, the customers had had enough. It wasn't as though the cockroaches and mice restricted themselves to storage or other hidden areas. No, left to their devices, the creatures gradually gained in confidence and audacity, scampering over the shelves during business hours and crawling out of

---

[1] Cf. spiegelonline.de, *Wenn der Paketbote gar nicht klingelt / When the postman doesn't ring at all,*
     20. August 2012

the toilet drains, sometimes taking a leisurely walk over the bistro counter. Even though reported in the local press, it was a long time before the 200-kilometer distant central office got wind of the infamy. (Which is why we immediately recommended generating a press clipping!) It took months before the branch manager's sabotage reached executive ears. He was, of course, immediately fired. It subsequently came to light that Georg had three company cars, but nary a driver's license…

During the first few months, the new branch manager also avoided shopping or eating at the store. The very thought turned his stomach. Understandably, when you think his first inspection turned up more than 60 dead mice, and over the next year he was obligated to get up at night twice weekly and open shop for the exterminators. The damage his predecessor had inflicted on customer relations wasn't as easily remedied. Regaining lost trust is always a painstaking process, especially in the foodstuffs and gastronomy areas. Effectively and ultimately successfully, we were able to help our client meet the challenge, which included establishing new, company-wide communication and information structures.

These examples clearly illustrate the significance of employee engagement. Which brings us to the reciprocity of the emotional bond outlined at the beginning of this chapter. If a business is to be successful, its leaders must do precisely that – they must lead. They must be a shining example of dedication and enthusiasm. And there lies the crux. Our extensive experience proves there is a massive deficit in true leaders. The repercussions are devastating, as studies show.

"Emotionally detached and ready to move on, every fifth employee is internally preparing to resign," is the result of the Gallup Engagement Index. The study also reveals, that commitment can be distinctively increased with the appropriate leadership approach. According to Gallup, direct superiors play the leading role, having a direct impact on employee fluctuation.[1] In many cases, employees do not abandon the company, they abandon their direct

---

[1] handwerk-magazin.de, *Gallup Engagement Index: Innere Kündigung vermeiden / Avoiding premeditated resignations*, 07.04.2014

bosses. In smaller companies, this can be one and the same person, but in larger enterprises, the choice of who's the boss is not to be underestimated. Boss-employee conflicts can sometimes be solved by a transfer to another department or team. When this is not feasible, the employee often has no other choice than to leave the company and seek another employer.

Yet, in these times of skilled worker shortage and demographic change, a company can no longer afford to lose its best employees. Furthermore, fluctuation is costly, resulting in lost knowledge and productivity, while training a staff member new to your company.

Showing the other side of the coin, the following example depicts a leadership style that negatively impacts, or even sabotages employee engagement. The enterprise in question is a Catholic clinic in Hessen, Germany which changed hands some years ago. Most of the workforce was thrilled to learn that they would keep their jobs, but their joy was short-lived. Soon after the take-over, a series of directives made clear that the new owners were solely interested in the clinic's economic aspects. They wanted to milk as much profit as possible by rejecting investments in new medical equipment and tightly clocking patient contact intervals. How the staff reacted to or applied these dictates was secondary, there was little or no personal communication on the matter. But the radical change of course soon caused mutinous murmuring among the staff, who neither could nor wanted to uphold the new values. While under the church's guidance, patient care and philanthropy were priorities. Now, under the new management, economy, efficiency and occupancy rates were all that mattered. (Read more on values in our books *D.R.E.A.M. of LEADERS® Leadership is not an Illusion*, as well as in *Workbook: Attitude*)

With Andreas, Dirk and Sandra, three leaders working at the clinic since its church days, we will demonstrate how a direct superior influences employee engagement. We will also introduce our four-square diagram on employee engagement:

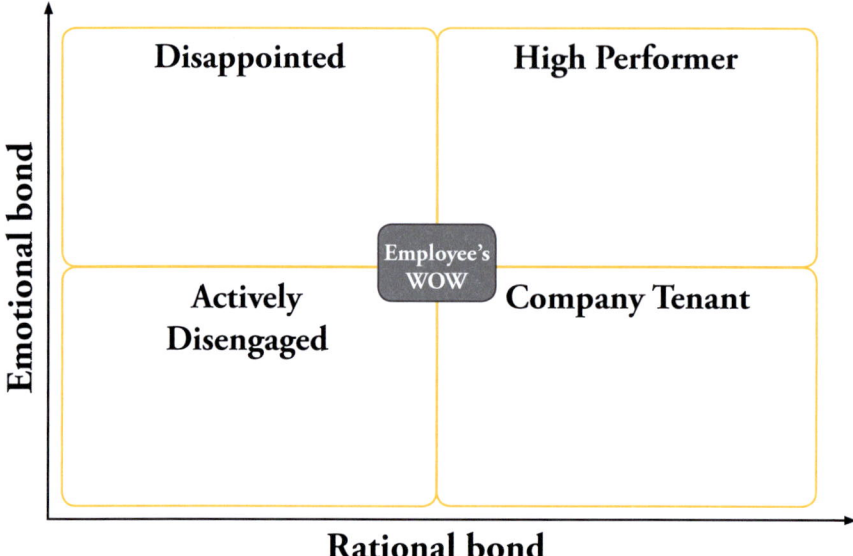

There are four different relationships branching out from the parameters rational and emotional attachment. We define an employee with a strong rational, and equally strong emotional, connection with his direct superior as an engaged employee, a high performer or a brand ambassador.

Andreas, the director of nursing at the now privatized clinic in Hessen, is such a high performer. He doesn't agree with many of the changes, yet his engagement remains steadfast. Andreas draws his motivation from his team, the people he leads, and not from his direct superiors, whose leadership methods do not offer him any source of orientation. It is only the collaboration with his team members that provides him with the motivation to continue performing well and with dedication.

Thus, he succeeds in creating a professional homeland for his employees, who were equally disoriented after the clinic changed hands. (The next chapter goes further into the topic of professional homeland.) Andreas works closely with his colleagues, enabling him to bring about the necessary restructuring in their interest. His drive to perform well is fueled by his employees' loyalty and admiration. This is an outstanding accomplishment for someone leading with passion yet led with indifference!

Dirk, the clinic's medical director, is just as unhappy with the new management as Andreas is. But Dirk is less able to ignore or offset his discontent and frustration since his motivation was always sustained by his direct superior, from his leader – which is impossible with the new management. The ethics and values projected outwardly are not in alignment with his bosses' leadership approach.

For Dirk, this contradiction is insupportable. Any and all of his suggestions or requests are consistently rejected by the new management. From Dirk's vantage point, he is denied the anticipated appreciation to which he had been accustomed throughout the many years of church sponsorship. Severely disappointed, Dirk's engagement takes a dive. This disappointment and frustration are characteristic of people with a powerful emotional bond with their company, yet an insignificant rational bond with their direct superiors. Dirk still loves his workplace, but the massive letdown leaves the question *"What am I still doing here?"* unanswered. The well of the emotional bond has run dry, and he is not equipped to answer the question rationally. So, with a heavy heart, Dirk leaves the clinic, or better, he leaves his direct superiors.

An employee with a strong rational, but paltry emotional bond with his employer is known as a company tenant or job-hopper. His motivation for working where he works is purely rational and the moment something better comes along, he has no difficulty cutting the cord. There's no love lost between him and his employer. It is comparable with a tenant's choice of apartment. As long as the place is rationally attractive – affordable rent, close to work – he'll stay. But as soon as an even more affordable or better situated apartment comes along, he'll move out without a second thought. An emotional person responds differently. He is so attached to his home and the nice neighbors, he wouldn't move, even if he was offered a less expensive apartment or one that halved his commuting distance.

At the Hessian clinic, Sandra was a job-hopper. When she realized that the new management wasn't going to be a bowl of cherries, she was neither disappointed like Dirk, nor did she compensate by focusing on her team, as Andreas did. Without an emotional bond with her workplace or with her superiors, she immediately began looking for an alternative, with success. First, she became ward director at a hospital in Erfurt, moving on only ten months later to a geriatric home in Nuremburg. When, about six months later, her former employer in Erfurt proposed a better offer, she returned for a year and a half. After a short sojourn of two months at a Thuringia health office, a higher salary moved her to accept an assessor position at a medical advisory services office in western Germany.

Apparently, soccer pro Dembélé's attachment to Borussia Dortmund (BVB) was also of a purely rational nature. After only one year in Dortmund, he received an offer from Barcelona. When BVB, refused to release him from his contract, Dembélé simply didn't show up for training, disappearing for days at a time. The club finally let their star player go, albeit under protest, demanding and receiving a record-breaking transfer fee, as was proudly announced at a press conference.

"They must have felt like a mere stepping stone, exploited by someone already harboring greater plans than Dortmund could offer. Dembélé says he has been a Barcelona fan since he was eight years old. While playing for Stade Rennes last summer, the Catalonians made him an offer, but he turned them down. 'I'd only been playing professionally for half a year.' It was too early on. Shortly thereafter, he came to Dortmund to play in the champion's league, '…playing an entire season with a good team, gathering more playtime and experience.' Doubtlessly, it worked."[1]

These are classic hallmarks of job-hoppers or company tenants. Since, from the start, they do not establish an emotional bond with their employer, they chose their positions according to purely rational criteria, with their minds solely focused on *what's in it for me*. A wholly legitimate approach.

At the same time, job-hoppers are not especially interested in a company's values, which certainly can be criticized. Such as the quality management leader working for a global sanitary supplier, who switched over to the arms industry. His motto, "If the money's right, I could care less about company values. It makes no difference to me whether I control the quality of heating valves or of tanks." A similar tactic applies to top politicians, who give the obligatory face-

---

[1] welt.de, *Als Dembélé sich entschied, den BVB zu erpressen / Dembélé decided to blackmail the BVB*, 04.09.2017.

time before seamlessly moving on to the lobby department of a company or association – often leaving a nasty taste in the public's mouth.

Fortunately, among the leaders at the Hessian clinic, none of them were both rationally and emotionally indifferent. In our four-square diagram, these are the actively disengaged employees, what we call want-away bomb plotters. These people do everything in their power to sabotage their employer or direct superior, and when they finally do go away, it's usually with a bang. Remember Georg, inflicting enormous damage not only on his employer's reputation, but also on the company's returns, by ignoring the mouse and cockroach infestation.

Key Lisciaman message
Leaders must forge ahead with engagement and enthusiasm for the task at hand. Only then will they find equally committed employees, who gladly develop into brand ambassadors.

Your notes

Worksheet: Your bond and that of your employees

Think about your bond to your employer. If you are independent, reflect on your bond to your profession, to your sphere of activity. Which of the four squares applies to you? And which emotional and rational factors shape your bond? If your bond is weak, what do you need to strengthen it? Write the answers below.

I see myself in the _____ square.

What shapes my rational bond?

_____
_____
_____

What contributes to my emotional bond?

_____
_____
_____

What is lacking on a rational level?

_____
_____
_____

What is lacking on an emotional level?

_____
_____
_____

Now, think about your employees! Who is in which of the four squares? Enter their names into the corresponding squares!

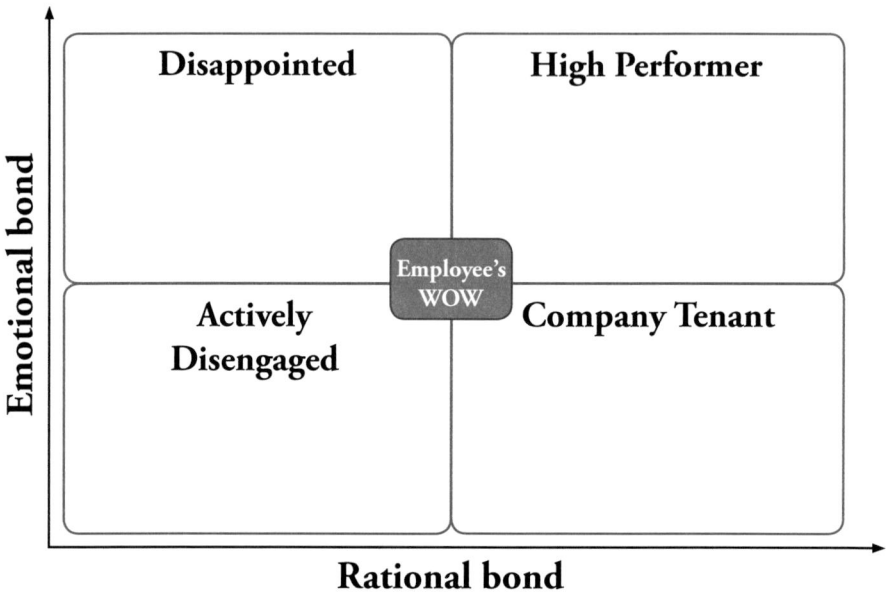

If you discover a weak emotional or rational bond in yourself or your employees, then probe into how you can strengthen the bond, defining concrete measures to carry out!

_____

_____

_____

_____

_____

_____

_____

_____

_____

CEO:	Naturally, our managers can also take part in leadership training sessions.
LISCIA:	Why is that? Will they soon be taking on leadership positions?
CEO:	They already have. They wouldn't be managers otherwise!
LISCIA:	And are the manager's employees led or managed?
CEO:	Come again?
LISCIA:	If you use the term manager, we should also talk about the term leader. These are two very different things.
CEO:	I never looked at it that way ...

Manager or Leader?

Attending to the direct superior's role within the company, and whether she interprets it correctly, is decisive. Does she see herself as a manager or as a leader? Does she act accordingly? The precise differentiation of these two positions is one of the first messages we put across in our leadership training sessions. Our experience reveals that many companies are wholly unaware of the far-reaching consequences a misinterpretation brings about.

They are oblivious to the threat it poses to their company or project. Management manages – structures, numbers, data and facts. You could also say management primarily governs the factual-rational and analytical aspects. A manager maintains processes and systems.

A *leader*, however, and this is the crux of the matter, works with *people*, for whom she is responsible. She is accountable for their well-being, as far as it is within her power. She is required to create an environment in which they enjoy working, can evolve further and advance their team. (Detailed information on this issue can be found in our books *D.R.E.A.M. of LEADERS® Leadership is not an Illusion* and *Workbook: Responsibility*)

To give you a concrete example taken from our experiences with this complex topic, let us introduce you to Christian, a more rational specimen who was once plant director at a northern Italian furniture manufacturer. There was already trouble brewing when Christian assumed the position, first and foremost in production with the rather older workforce. One problem was an addition to the product portfolio. A new, luxury series of lounge chairs, the standard model being upholstered in fabric, were to be covered in leather. Not an unsolvable dilemma, but still requiring more effort, as working with leather demanded more physical strength than textiles did. The, on the average, older production staff therefore needed more time to produce one chair than the company had calculated, much more time. The team lagged far behind the expected production tempo.

Plant director Christian's problem, though, was on another plane. He managed the factory almost wholly from his office, avoiding contact with the workers from the word go. He remained an unknown entity for his employees. The bulk of his communication was via email, or he called individual workers into his office instead of making the occasional trip to production to see the lay of the land for himself, listening to the workers' assessment of the problem. Christian is a manager per se, a man concerned with indexes and Excel tables, comparing data offered by the factory computer. These, not the people actually doing the work, were his decision-making methods and tools.

Of course, it didn't take long for the floodgates of accusation to burst open, claiming Christian was incompetent, unequipped to aptly communicate with his employees. Especially the older production workers were urgently in need of personal attention from their superior. There were many among them with disability IDs issued by the company physician, restricting activities due to, for example, a chronic illness or a weak back. These ID holders were prohibited from carrying out certain production tasks. This was one of the reasons the leather lounge chair model production proceeded at a snail's pace. And Christian actually believed he could solve these massive people-related problems from his desk chair, instead of seeking them out personally.

So, even though he listened to the accusations against him, it remained unclear as to whether he granted them validity. Unfortunately, we had very little time to work with Christian before he was transferred to a factory in China as a launch manager – certainly not enough time to help him make a substantial change. Thus, we were skeptical that the transfer would solve the furniture manufacturer's problems with their plant director, as launch managers, responsible for introducing new markets for all plants, must also work with people.

Unfortunately, lack of insight into the two terms *leader* and *manager* often results in leadership positions being filled by the wrong people. Thus, we periodically broach the subject in companies, "You hire a manager and send her off to master a leadership development program when what you really need is a leader. Have you ever considered hiring a leader and sending her to a management skills seminar?" Even in human resources departments, our line of thought often causes astonishment, as if we were out of touch with reality.

All the same, when taking a closer look, it turns out that the same errant placements had been made in the past, repeatedly. We then advise such enterprises to rethink their future recruiting strategy, examining more closely just who they take on for which position. Certainly, mistakes happen, but repeating the same mistake is avoidable. As Albert Einstein put it, "Insanity: doing the same thing repeatedly and expecting different results."

Therefore, HR departments should pay more attention to the skills required for a certain position. Do you need a manager or a leader? Instead, they only look at the candidate's trade-specific knowledge and experience. Of course, it is advantageous if a candidate has, for example, worked in Brazil for five years. Foreign experience always looks good on a résumé, although it rarely states whether the person had a leading or managing role. A more significant question is what that person's precise duties were in Brazil, and whether they are relevant to the position you are looking to fill in your company.

The work with our furniture manufacturer in northern Italy instilled an innovative approach. Christian's successor was Matteo, a man we consider the prototype for D.R.E.A.M. Leaders. In his previous position at another factory, Matteo was well-versed in the problems that can emerge in production. The decisive argument for hiring him as plant director, however, was the ease with which he moved from the world of management to the world of leadership. Matteo could read, compile and demand the fulfillment of criteria, while constantly aware that in the final analysis these indicators would be realized by people. On his first day at the plant, he immediately went to the people he would be working with and spoke with them. Within a brief period of time, he knew every co-worker and their needs. He was in a position to respond to each of them individually, instilling trust and thus, the basis for good, successful collaboration. When defining the difference between these two distinct roles and their responsibilities, we like to use the following analogy: Leaders are responsible for providing a professional home for their employees; a piece of Earth where they feel comfortable and productive. The manager, on the other hand, builds the house on the land, since without a roof over one's head it's hard to feel at home. Both functions should work hand in hand. A company needs both a manager and a leader, so categorizing the two into stronger/weaker; better/worse is utter nonsense. The only important thing is to define very clearly which aspects are required for which position.

Yet not every enterprise has the financial means to hire two people. Above all, in small and mid-sized companies, the roles of leader and manager must often be enacted by one and the same player, even if he would rather concentrate on the one or the other. We often think of Denise in this context, a boutique owner in downtown Potsdam, who sought us out because, as she so aptly put it, she "simply wasn't getting ahead." Our analysis revealed that Denise was an in-the-flesh leader. Her daily encounters with the people in her shop – both co-workers and customers – was her passion and her talent. Staff, customers and suppliers praised her to the skies and sales returns were also satisfactory. With her infallible instinct for style and trends, her boutique in the Potsdam pedestrian zone should have been a gold mine.

And it would have been if Denise had had a better grasp of numbers and was better organized on the whole. To be perfectly blunt, Denise was about as management savvy as a mushroom. And she admitted it freely when we asked. Her basement was full of stock – not from the current season, but from the preceding years. Ergo, out of fashion and basically unsaleable.

Being Denise, a warm-hearted person, loved by employees, customers and suppliers alike, we had no desire to turn her inside out. All she needed was a few management skills, which we were more than happy to supply her with. We trained her in establishing an index system, a balanced scorecard, as well as in developing strategies. (More on the balanced scorecard in the last chapter of this workbook)

We also recommended a regular, seasonal sale to keep her basement from overflowing with stock that in the end, would be written off as a loss. Without too much effort, Denise was able distinctly improve her credit column. We also helped her to understand that customer kindness and fair dealing have their economic limits. Denise could no longer afford to take back boots a customer bought over a year ago. Even though the goods were in excellent condition, they were from the past season and thusly unsaleable in a boutique specializing in the latest fashions.

Although, in the beginning, Denise insisted that numbers and management were simply not her thing, she applied the measures we worked out together well, contributing many of her own ideas. She was highly motivated, especially as she quickly saw her efforts paying off. Before our collaboration, she would never have thought she could be a leader *and* (at least in some areas) a manager, not in her wildest dreams.

Linguistically, a manager is a person who handles or directs things, such as resources. A manager organizes, carries out or delegates the how, where and when of any structured system, she is responsible for a smoothly running system or company. A leader, on the other hand, guides or directs people and ideas. A leader is responsible for the people within the system or company. Just as the two terms are differentiated in the English language, both are equally valuable components, as they should be in any company, structure or system.

Hence, the first and most decisive question is, "What am I really? Do I lead, or do I manage?" When we speak of dedication, we are not speaking of dedication to management. The D.R.E.A.M. of LEADERS deals with dedication to people work, working with and on the human beings who are dependent on you and your function. The difference between leader and manager is not hierarchical, yet there *is* a difference and it has a significant impact on your company's success. Numbers can be managed – people can't. People must be led.

But not from a desk or per email. This leadership approach earned plant manager Christian a transfer to China, a transfer he didn't want. Had he refused, though, he would have lost his job. His superiors gave him very little choice in the matter.

But Christian is not a singularity. The precise difference between leadership and management, including its multifarious impacts, is unfortunately still a rare insight, far from being common knowledge. Our clients, regardless of the sector, whether it's a "rational" area, i.e. automobile supplier or technology business, or a so-called "social" enterprise, i.e. elderly care or hospital, generally assume that people can be handled like machines. In our training sessions with the latter, we often hear staff members speak of colleagues in the same terms as an auto supplier speaks of a machine's capacity. Even though it should be more than obvious to any sentient being that there is an enormous difference between bi-weekly machine maintenance and a geriatric nurse's eventual incapacity to "function" properly.

Furthermore, managers may work ten, 12 or 14 hours day, but when the work is done, they go home. Leaders are leaders through and through. Leading is an inner conviction, lived 24/7 or not lived at all. Leaders are born. They are leaders in kindergarten, become class representatives at school or team captains at the sports club. A leader is president of the dove breeders' society or a youth sports trainer. But in your company, they often stand on the production line or run facilities. They're doing an excellent job, no doubt about it. Yet they are plagued by a nagging dissatisfaction because they are not following their true calling – leading people. This can eventually turn into deep frustration, diminishing or destroying their company commitment.

Abraham Maslow, U.S. American psychologist and founder of the *hierarchy of needs*, aptly describes this condition, "Capacities clamor to be used, and cease their clamor only when they are well used. That is, capacities are also needs."[1]

There is plenty of dormant leadership potential in companies, because managers have no idea with whom they are working day in, day out. Managers have no idea which potential lies fallow in their co-workers. And, why should they? It's not in their job description, and it surely isn't their responsibility. That's what a leader should do.

When we say a leader is a leader 24/7, we don't mean she's supposed to work 24/7, we mean she is a leader, in her blood, her muscle and in her inner attitude toward commitment. Leadership is the expression of her humanity. She cannot take it off when she goes home at the end of a work day. Uli Hoeneß is an excellent example of inherent leadership. After sitting out his prison sentence

---

[1] Maslow, Abraham H., *Toward a Psychology of Being*, Start Publishing eBook Edition, pg.337

for tax evasion, he is once more president of the FC Bayern München soccer club. Life without this club (and his leadership role) is unimaginable. "Hoeneß is only happy when he is doing what he has been doing with commitment and passion for the last 47 years, leading the fate of FC Bayern [...] He thinks FC Bayern, feels FC Bayern, he is FC Bayern – 24 hours a day, seven days a week, 365 days a year, his lifelong," Chairman Karl-Heinz Rummenigge declares.[1]

---

[1] bild.de, *Happy Birthday, Uli Hoeneß*, 04.01.2017

Key Lisciaman message
Leaders create a professional homeland
for their employees, while managers
build the house to shelter them.
Neither is more or less vital – leaders
and managers must work hand in hand,
their positions crystal clearly defined
within the company.

Your notes

Worksheet: Manager or leader? A self-assessment

How do I rate myself as a leader on a scale from 1 to 10? (1 = not at all, 10 = absolutely)

1   2   3   4   5   6   7   8   9   10

Using the same scale, how satisfied am I with my leadership rating (1 = not at all, 10 = absolutely)?

1   2   3   4   5   6   7   8   9   10

Now, rate yourself as a manager (1 = not at all, 10 = absolutely).

1   2   3   4   5   6   7   8   9   10

Using the same scale, how satisfied am I with my manager rating? (1 = not at all, 10 = absolutely satisfied)

1   2   3   4   5   6   7   8   9   10

If you would like to further develop your leadership (or managerial) skills, and are rather dissatisfied with your rating, then define below five measures to help you improve your rating:

1   _____

_____

_____

2   _____

_____

_____

3 _____

_____

_____

4 _____

_____

_____

5 _____

_____

_____

CEO:	If there were only a way to measure how good or how poorly my leaders lead.
LISCIA:	There is.
CEO:	Nothing complicated, you know, clear results giving a maximum of seven rankings.
LISCIA:	Five'll do it.
CEO:	And it shows me where each of them needs to invest his energies to become a better leader?
LISCIA:	Precisely.

D.R.E.A.M.-Score®

The preceding chapter made perfectly clear the importance of differentiating between manager and leader. But defining is not enough. We want to give our clients a solid, practical tool for measuring the leadership quality of their company managers. This was the driving force behind developing the D.R.E.A.M.-Score®.

The D.R.E.A.M.-Score® comprises 25 questions based on the five D.R.E.A.M. of LEADERS categories – Dedication, Responsibility, Education, Attitude and Motivation. The person holding a leading position answers the questions and receives a point score based on his responses. Direct co-workers also answer the same 25 questions in reference to their boss. Thus, both a self-assessment and an external assessment are generated and given points.

The D.R.E.A.M.-Score® results subdivide leadership qualities into the following groups: "Learner" (0-50 points), "Prospective Manager" (51-70 points), "Manager" (71-80 points), "Leading Manager" (81-90 points) and "D.R.E.A.M. Leader" (91-100 points). Each group is given recommendations, enabling managerial staff to become "D.R.E.A.M. Leaders."

"Learner" (0-50 points)
You are just setting out on the path to discover your strengths. An assessment would help you to examine your leadership disposition.
"Prospective Manager" (51-70 points)
You are an aspiring manager. Consider a coaching or mentoring process to

reflect on and examine your attitude and values. Thus, you can make a conscious decision whether your future career lies in management or leadership.

"Manager" (71-80 points)

You are a manager, a trade-specific and disciplinary leader. Consider a coaching or mentoring process to reflect on and examine your attitude and values. Thus, you can make a conscious, personal decision whether your future career continues along managerial lines or takes you toward leadership.

"Leading Manager" (81-90 points)

In addition to classic managerial tasks (maintaining processes and systems), you also have a predilection and talent for leadership (people work). You are able to transform visions into viable perspectives, pointing the way and guiding people along this path. You are only one step away from becoming a D.R.E.A.M. Leader. Keep going!

D.R.E.A.M. Leader (91-100 points)

Congratulations, you have the stuff D.R.E.A.M. Leaders are made of! You know your organization inside and out and are well acquainted with the people you work with. You think long-term and act accordingly. Your guiding principle, "You are not a leader until you have cultivated the power to lead that can cultivate leadership power in others."

We developed the D.R.E.A.M.-Score® by carrying out a five-month study with over 550 managerial staff and employees from 20 European countries and the U.S.A. The results were enlightening. Although the average D.R.E.A.M.-Score® of managerial staff members' self-assessment moved between "Manager" with tendencies to "Leading Manager," direct employees evaluated them no stronger than "Prospective Manager."

We have broken down the discrepancy as it was revealed in the five categories.

In the category Dedication, managerial staff gave themselves an average of 77.8 points, placing them as "Manager" with a tendency toward "Leading Manager." Their employees agreed that they were "Managers," but the awarded average 71.9 points placed them just a hair above "Prospective Manager."

Looking at the Responsibility category, the discrepancy intensifies. Here, managerial staff gave themselves an average of 79.9 points, at the high end of the "Manager" group, only 1.1 points from the "Leading Manager" group. Their employees, however, viewed them as "Prospective Manager," giving only an average of 69.8 points.

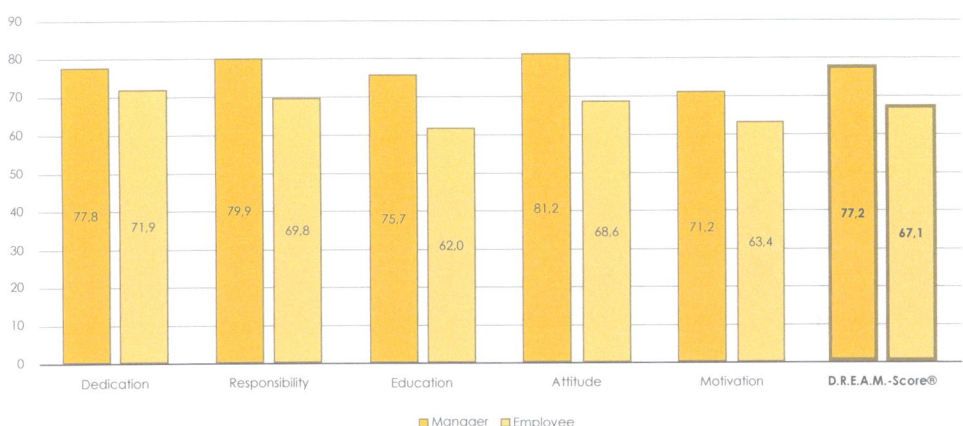

In the Education area, self-assessments averaged 75.7 points ("Manager"), while employee ratings averaged a mere 62 points ("Prospective Manager"). This tendency held steady when assessing the issue of Attitude. The managerial staff considered themselves "Leading Managers" at an average of 81.2 points. Direct employees took a completely different view, averaging their boss' leadership qualities in Attitude at 68.6 points, i.e. as "Prospective Managers."

A similar study discrepancy arose in the category Motivation. The managerial staff's rating of 71.2 points lay markedly above their employees' rating of 63.4.

Evidently, the D.R.E.A.M.-Score® is an extremely efficient and useful method for analyzing leadership and management qualities. The varying results reveal a company's strengths and weaknesses, enabling them to directly address and optimize deficient areas with supplementary measures.

By the way, it is a rare specimen unifying the qualities of a leader and manager in one human body, oscillating between one and the other on command. Over the many years of working in the area, we have met several "Leading Managers," and have developed numerous, as well. But as for "D.R.E.A.M. Leaders," well, there are a handful out there…

Key Lisciaman message
Would you like to try out the
D.R.E.A.M.-Score® on yourself?
Then write to:
Dream-Score@Liscia-Consulting.com,
where you can order access
and receive more information.

Your notes

Worksheet: How do you rate your own leadership qualities?

Where do you stand in reference to the D.R.E.A.M. Formula[1]? Rate yourself using the scale below (1 = none at all, 10 = top of the ladder) to attain an initial result for your orientation!

Dedication	1	2	3	4	5	6	7	8	9	10
Responsibility	1	2	3	4	5	6	7	8	9	10
Education	1	2	3	4	5	6	7	8	9	10
Attitude	1	2	3	4	5	6	7	8	9	10
Motivation	1	2	3	4	5	6	7	8	9	10

Now, add the single values and divide by 5.
What is the final sum? _____

Result

0-3	=	Learner
4-5	=	Prospective Manager
6-7	=	Manager
8-9	=	Leading Manager
10	=	D.R.E.A.M. Leader

For a more precise result, following the above Key Lisciaman message!

---

[1] D.R.E.A.M.-Formel® is a protected trademark owned by Liscia Consulting and registered with the German Patent and Trademark Office.

CEO:	Here it is – just let me dust it off a bit – this is the folder with all our collected visions. It's all in there.
LISCIA:	I see, it's all in that folder.
CEO:	That's right. Anyone who wants to know why we're doing what we do, can read it here in black and white.
LISCIA:	The folder doesn't look particularly well-thumbed.
CEO:	Nope, it looks pretty new.
LISCIA:	So, everyone already knows why you're launching the change?
CEO:	I'm not so sure about that.
LISCIA:	You should be!
CEO:	You mean, I should let people know where the folder is?
LISCIA:	No. As CEO, your workforce needs to hear from you why they should want to, why they need to go through the transition with you. You must answer their questions and speak to their hearts.
CEO:	Speak to their hearts?
LISCIA:	Yes, to their hearts.

Future visions

A leader radiates commitment throughout her environment, painting a vision of the future – indispensable to employee engagement. Of course, managers also have visions, albeit ones differing from those of leaders in one major aspect – a manager's vision is more rational, more in terms of a goal, while a leader's vision is a clear directive on the future. Here's an example:

When a system catering business intends to increase its number of restaurants to 200 in Germany, a dedicated manager immediately begins to calculate numbers and compile data in her mind.

In a leader's mind's eye, an entire vista unfolds, depicting the business's successful future. She visualizes it; is emotionally inspired by it, and this emotion, this passion, is what galvanizes her enthusiasm. And this enthusiasm infects her employees, until each one has their own unclouded vision of, in this case, opening the 200th restaurant. Or in the words of the French author Antoine de Saint-Exupéry, "If you want to build a ship, don't drum up the men to gather wood, divide the work and give orders (manager). Instead, teach them to yearn for the vast and endless sea (leader)."

The manager's primary question is, "*What* do we want to achieve?" The leader poses a different key question, "*Why* do we want to achieve this?" The leader's drive to visualize the answer to this question himself, before infusing her employees with purpose, allows them, too, to find the answer to the question, "Yes, why *are* we doing this?" – this is what we call *Dedication*.

Every vision takes shape personally and individually. A vision cannot be handed down or passed on from a superior or colleague without reflecting on its content. A vision must suit me to a tee, otherwise, it has no power.

Realizing this was an enormous relief to Natalia, a leader at a mid-sized metal working and surface technology company. When we asked her what her vision was at the beginning of our coaching, she was visibly discomfited, replying, "I was afraid you would ask me that. These damned visions plague me...I'm constantly asked about my vision, but I haven't the foggiest idea what I should say. I just don't have one, although everyone's supposed to have a vision, at least that's what people say. It's so embarrassing. All my colleagues can reel off their visions at the drop of a hat – house, Porsche, boat – I'm the only one who's clueless. It's one of my major failings. Without a vision, I don't know which direction to take, right?"

The first two misconceptions we cleared out of Natalia's way was that a vision didn't have to be earth-shaking, and that it was primarily a deeply personal view. We then asked her to think about the following questions, leaving a pause after each one. *Why do I go to work every day? – What does my work give me? – Why do I accept all the stress and extra hours? – Why do I carry this load so willingly?* We could see Natalia cogitating and then, beaming, she suddenly exclaimed, "If that's the case, then I do have a vision!" She then told us that her major motivation was to give her daughter a good education. "You see, I also went to college, but it was hard road, full of privations. My father died when I was young, and money was always incredibly tight. So, I really had to fight my way through to get where I am today. I want it to be easier for my daughter. I want her to be able to concentrate solely on her studies without constantly worrying about money."

For Natalia, this conversation was both enlightening and a great relief. She realized she didn't lack anything at all. She had always had a vision, she just didn't know it by name. She was convinced (or had been convinced) that a vision had to be something huge, a holiday home on the Virgin Islands, at the very least! She had been so busy comparing herself with her colleagues, she forgot to focus on herself and her individual situation. It became clear to her that a good, unburdened education for her daughter was reason enough to go to work each day. And if that's not something huge, we don't know what is.

When it comes to visions, companies like to think in Olympic dimensions, higher! faster! further! Whether it's right for the company or its employees is often disregarded. Thus, we often hear visions like, "We will lead the market by the end of the year!" or "We will double our workforce over the next five years, earning the highest returns on the sector!" Still, a vision can also be to lead a successful enterprise where happy, satisfied employees find their professional homeland. The strategy extracted from this vision could be, "We will remain mid-sized, even in the future. Expanding would also mean adopting corporate structures, at the cost of our familial environment. Hence, expansion could easily mean we could no longer ensure that our workers feel at home here." Too simple? Too sentimental? Not ambitious enough? *Why not?*

Then let's take another example. Three executives of a small, successfully positioned consulting enterprise haven't the blurriest vision of amassing as many advisors as possible, zooming around the planet form them. That just doesn't fit. Their vision is to merely develop five successors who are equally dedicated carrying on to their ideas, so that one day they can happily retire. (Similarities with living persons such as those authoring this book are purely coincidental and certainly not intentional…)

So, you see, visions do not have to take on mammoth proportions. A vision is your imagined future, triggering emotions like happiness, contentment and pride (the latter a rare commodity in Germany).

The American actor Matthew McConaughey appears to have had his future vision at very early age. In his acceptance speech upon being awarded the Oscar® in 2014, he said when he was 15 years old, someone asked him who his role model, his hero was. McConaughey asked for two weeks to think it over, finally answering, "It´s me in ten years."[1] Ten years later, the same person

---

1   Quotes from our own recording of McConaughey's speech on March 2, 2014.

approached him, assuming the actor had now reached his goal. McConaughey disagreed. He hadn't even come close, because his vision consistently moved ten years further in the future. "So, you see every day, every week, every month and every year of my life, my hero is always ten years away. [...] And that's just fine with me because that keeps me with somebody to keep on chasing."

His guiding principle has always been, "Where do I want to be in ten years and what do I have to do to get there?" This is his vision. McConaughey neither aspires to be a role model for others, nor find someone else to be his mirror. Instead, he places himself ten years in the future and strives to emulate the vision of himself.

That is a very interesting method, that obviously works for Matthew McConaughey. He's been applying this vision for decades with evident success. All the same, we would like to point out that along with an image of the future, a view of the past is indispensable to assessing the shape of my (professional) self in the future. We call this the *reverse gap*, which you can read more about in the chapter *A – Attitude* in our book *D.R.E.A.M. of LEADERS® Leadership is not an Illusion*, as well in as the corresponding workbook.

Just like, Natalia, Matthew McConaughey found his own, deeply personal vision. It's not about more money, fame or recognition. His motivating force is the vision of himself in ten years.

Projecting this image onto your company, a vision of the future is not rational, factual plans to meet a projected goal, not by a long shot. It is the living vision that lets employees know where they are going and how success feels. It is the leader's responsibility to transfer not only her own purpose to her team, but to ensure that every person involved finds their own, personal purpose; their own, personal *why*. Just as every business is founded on and guided by its initiator's vision, each co-worker needs her own vision dovetailing with the company's. Otherwise, you run the risk of losing valuable people-power along the way. Should one of your team wake up one fine morning and ask himself, "Why am I doing this?" without finding a plausible answer, he will bring precisely this lack of enthusiasm to work with him.

Often, when we come into a company, we find, yes, there is a vision. It's been neatly typed up and filed. And is collecting dust on some storage shelf.

And the bigger the company, the greater the probability that the vision was formulated by top executives, usually with the help of a marketing agency. Beautifully crafted works of art, these visions are a joy to read, but for the employees doing the real work, they are nothing but empty phrases, without meaning or impact. Not very inspiring or motivating.

The same goes for the visions of Natalia's colleagues. They mean nothing to her simply because they are not *hers*. And donning others' visions is as authentically motivating as tying a hamburger in front of the donkey, instead of the delectable carrot.

A prefab vision could serve as a basis for discussion among the various departments. You could all examine its meaning and attempt to extract a viable vision from it to inspire you, your department or, when you work in a large corporation, for your entire business. Perhaps you could do this, but it is not an ideal solution.

Key Lisciaman message
Leaders have a sharp vision of the
future, passing the associated emotions
on to their employees, inspiring them
to find their own vision. A vision must
be *mine* if it is to guide me.

Your notes

Worksheet: How do you see the future? What drives you?

What is your vision?

_____
_____
_____
_____
_____

What clear image of the future triggers elation in you?

_____
_____
_____
_____
_____

What propels you forward?

_____
_____
_____
_____

Why?

_____
_____
_____
_____

CEO:	Of course, we have a company strategy!
LISCIA:	Excellent! And how is it transferred onto your leadership strategy?
CEO:	You mean a strategy for how our leaders should lead?
LISCIA:	Exactly.
CEO:	Do we really need one?
LISCIA:	You certainly do need one if we are agreed that your leaders should make a decisive contribution in applying your company strategy to and with their teams!
CEO:	Of course, they should!
LISCIA:	Then you need a leadership strategy in alignment with your company strategy.
CEO:	Why hasn't anyone told me this before?

First things first! A leadership strategy

Here, we come back to the leader, as it is his banner behavior that creates an optimal work environment for his employees. Yet, initial meetings at most companies reveal that they have no leadership strategy at all. Of course, decision-makers have usually given much thought and consideration to formulating a company strategy, defining the track they will take to future destinations. But rarely do they derive a leadership strategy from the results.

If this is the case, we first develop a binding leadership strategy together with company leaders. We probe into what company leaders want to achieve by leading. This is the first mandatory step toward aligning our training and measures precisely and accordingly. Once this is defined, we draw up a leadership philosophy, leadership mission, leadership values and leadership responsibilities.

Only then do we move on to establish practicalities. Here, we work out precise parameters for objectives or for key figures to evaluate our measures' success in one, two or three years. Key figures could refer to reducing defective goods or absenteeism, to boosting effectivity, decreasing employee fluctuation and increasing employee engagement. If the company has not applied these within the agreed upon time frame and is only interested in booking "some kind of seminar," then we are the wrong address. We are not here to give conventional seminars or training sessions. We are not all-round coaches. We are consultants who coach and train leaders.

An important instrument in our work is the so-called balanced scorecard, a kind of indications map in which the four legs: finances, customers, stakeholders and processes, must be in balance. The balanced scorecard connects strategy development to strategy application, or in other words, it is a concept for measuring, documenting and monitoring a company's activities in accord with its vision and strategy. The balanced scorecard was developed by a research team in the United States.

"Due to increasing criticism of the one-dimensional accent on financial indexes in the USA, R.S. Kaplan und D.P. Norton led a research team in the early nineties, studying twelve US American businesses. The objective was to adjust existing index systems to encompass the companies' heightened demands."[1]

Practically applied, the balanced scorecard defines the impacts on finances, customers, stakeholders and processes when a new process is introduced. What does this mean for stakeholders, i.e. the employees or suppliers? Are they equipped with the resources to carry the process through, or do they need training? If such is the case, then the impact on finances must be inspected. Should the customers also be affected by the process or change, then they must be informed prior to launching the process. How should this be done, per email or over the phone? That brings us back to the stakeholders – are there enough staff members to inform customers or do you need to recruit more? This would have financial consequences. Thus, when I launch a measure in one of the four areas, I must examine the repercussions on the other three areas and any consequences, along with the pertinent steps to take, are entered. The balanced scorecard is only completed when a measure has no more consequences.

The method is best explained with a concrete example. Imagine a specialized epicurean operating a popular, non-franchised restaurant destination seating 160 to 170 guests indoors and about 300 outdoors. His strategic objective is a new, pepped-up and more youthful menu. Our gourmet considers his plan a success when he gains 30 percent more guests between 21 and 39 years old, while losing only 10 percent of those under 21 and over 39. His focus on the age group 21 to 39 stems from his conviction that this group will spend the most money per person.

---

[1] https://www.investopedia.com/terms/b/balancedscorecard.asp

The first measure falls under the area of processes. A project team is to be created, made up of internal staff members from the restaurant and external advisors. The project team's initial act, of course, is to draft, define and adopt a project plan. This raises the primary question of the project team's budget (finance leg), composed of internal staff salaries and the costs for the external advisors.

Another important project team factor is the internal staff members' capacities and abilities. Are they thoroughly capable of carrying through with the project (stakeholders leg)? For those lacking the necessary skills, an applicable schooling must take place. Consequently, finances must be augmented to include training costs and the organization of said project management training must be entered in processes.

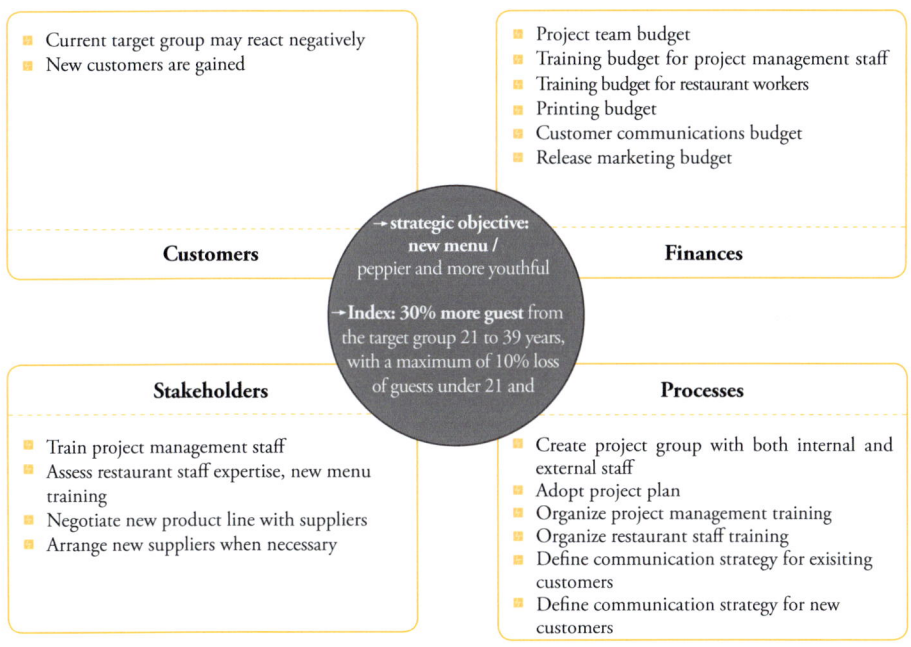

Customers
- Current target group may react negatively
- New customers are gained

Finances
- Project team budget
- Training budget for project management staff
- Training budget for restaurant workers
- Printing budget
- Customer communications budget
- Release marketing budget

→ strategic objective: new menu / peppier and more youthful

→ Index: 30% more guest from the target group 21 to 39 years, with a maximum of 10% loss of guests under 21 and

Stakeholders
- Train project management staff
- Assess restaurant staff expertise, new menu training
- Negotiate new product line with suppliers
- Arrange new suppliers when necessary

Processes
- Create project group with both internal and external staff
- Adopt project plan
- Organize project management training
- Organize restaurant staff training
- Define communication strategy for exisiting customers
- Define communication strategy for new customers

The first stage is reached when the menu is perfected. Now, restaurant staff must be clued in and taken along. How will we inform 60 to 70 staff members about the new menu? Another schooling is necessary, which must also be organized (processes) and the costs calculated (finances), or do we need a budget for this staff training?

Creating a new menu brings further stakeholder aspects to light. With the new menu, comes new ingredients and products. Hence, new arrangements must be made with suppliers. It may be necessary to work with completely different suppliers, who must be sought and found (processes). And, naturally, a menu must be printed, so we need a budget for printing costs (finances).

The customer leg of the balanced scorecard must also be considered. How will the new menu effect destination restaurant guests? The current target group, predominantly under 21 and over 39 years, could shun the change. Therefore, we need a communication strategy (processes) for the existing clientele, as well as a budget for customer communications (finances). The proprietor's intention, however, is to gain new customers, requiring thought on how potential guests aged 21 to 39 will learn of the new offer. Processes must come up with a customer strategy for new guests, as indeed finances must define a budget for marketing purposes.

This example makes perfectly clear that the simple act of creating a new, pepped-up, more youthful menu triggers a comprehensive catalog of measures. The advantage of a balanced scorecard lies in its straightforward illustration of the four legs: finances, stakeholders, customers and processes. It avoids nasty surprises during running processes. Our experience shows that most company projects fail due to a lack of thorough planning. It is much more efficient to take the time to plan intensively and to invest money in carrying it out properly in measured steps. Subsequent improvements or amendments, as all human experience shows, are not only costly but cause needless stress.

Should the proprietor neglect to plan a staff training, the day the new menu is launched, they are uninformed and under enormous pressure. Since they are occupied with learning the menu themselves, they are incapable of advising guests or answering their questions. The house is full, inside and out, of hungry guests, business could be great, but his staff confuses the numbers and names of the new meals, taking ages to get the orders right. And then there's mix-ups. Guests are brought meals they didn't order. Many are so fed up with the poor service, they won't set foot in the place (nor recommend it) again. The new menu is fine, the planning a disaster. Or think about the furniture manufacturer in northern Italy, who wanted to offer his lounge chair in a luxurious leather model. If those responsible had planned the measure with a balanced scorecard, they would have certainly noticed that what seems like a minor shift in materials would have massive impact on their employees. Without the appropriate communication and information strategy, such process adjustments are doomed to fail. This is where a leader's farsightedness is needed. When a process is to be altered, it is his responsibility to make sure adequate planning takes place first, enabling his staff to join the bandwagon, not fall off it.

In addition, we would like to make perfectly clear that personnel and leadership are two very different things. Relatively often, a CEO will tell us, "We're very active in our HR department, we have the topic leadership well covered."

That is a common fallacy. Human relations departments deal primarily with workers' rights, the Industrial Constitution Act, recruitment and dismissals, absentee analysis and personnel administration. They are managers; they organize. Correspondingly, it is the leaders who are responsible for their employees' development, not human relations.

You can read more about this in the chapter *E – Education* in our book *D.R.E.A.M. of LEADERS® Leadership is not an Illusion*, as well as in the corresponding workbook. We are most decidedly not intending to play down the role of personnel managers, rather to ensure a clear distribution of responsibilities. Should a leader wish to develop a particular employee, he must communicate with HR, who, among other things, check to see if there's a budget or whether an external specialist is required.

We are convinced that our work must begin at the top, with a company's executives, board of directors or at least its department managers. We know it makes no sense to invest energies in the production line, training a group leader on how to best motivate and lead his co-workers when there is no shining example radiating from the executive level. This would only result in a (frustrated) group leader applying what he has learned, only to have the boss come and say, "What do you think you're doing? We don't have time for such nonsense!"

So, obviously, we bring our knowledge to the executive level. There is an adage aptly describing this situation, *The fish rots from the head down*. Problems, crises and non-productivity – these are failings often triggered by people at the top of the hierarchy. Our experience confirms this. Defective leadership can bring a company to the brink of destruction. Its foundation crumbles as unmotivated employees become clock-watchers, while considering resigning or even sabotage.

But you can also turn it around, *The sun shines from above*. A leader with the right strategy and the license to express his commitment to and passion for guiding people, will broadcast the firelight of his enthusiasm throughout the entire concern without diminishing its warmth or radiance. He will bring out the best in himself and his team, leading the business to success, even in the toughest of times.

Key Lisciaman message
Drawing on the company strategy, a leadership strategy must be developed. Only when the executive level lives and breathes certain values, will they be taken for granted further down in the hierarchy.

Your notes

Worksheet: Your leadership strategy

1. Formulate the goal leadership should achieve in your company!

_____

_____

_____

_____

_____

2. What is your leadership philosophy (fundamental stance, guideline)?

_____

_____

_____

3. What is your leadership mission (objective and assignment)?

_____

_____

_____

4. What are your leadership values (i.e. openness, communication, respect, etc)?

_____

_____

_____

5. Which practical leadership task do you derive from question 1 to 4?

_____

_____

_____

The Authors

Marcello, Gianni and Jan Liscia (left to right)

Since its inception in 2000, taking shape in Paderborn, Germany, the name *Liscia Consulting* has gained ground on both national and international terrain with their excellent work in leader development. A most competent partner for strategy, conception and getting things done.

Business leaders Gianni, Marcello and Jan Liscia are not your everyday seminar conductors. Nor are they generic trainers or coaches. Gianni, Marcello and Jan Liscia are consultants who train and coach *leaders*. They are strategic partners, guiding and mediating transitional processes.

www.Liscia-Consulting.com

Keynote presentations for your event

On the pulse of change with inspiring keynote lectures! A keynote presentation can be designed to run 30 minutes or up to 3 hours – according to your event's agenda!

Together, we determine the focus of your D.R.E.A.M. of LEADERS® keynote lecture, i.e. Employee Engagement in Global Leadership, Transitional Process Leadership or Digital Leadership. Our multifarious and unusual approach infuses your business with new impulses, creating an atmosphere of awakening and a desire for change.

A rational/emotional composition coupled with the blunt, stark reality of our times invokes profound reflection. To easier digest discomfiting truth, we served it with a healthy portion of humor.

One 'n' Herman, the artist

Herman, illustrator

Herman is, and has been for some time, one of the most high-profile, successful pop art painters of our time. His edgy, idiosyncratic graphics and pictures are downright bodacious. Once a trained screen printer, his unleashed creativity has astonished viewers at over 200 national and international exhibits. Herman has been an independent artist since 1991.

Over the past years, the name Herman can also be found under cartoons drawn for a variety of German publishing houses. His *flying heart* comic strip in *Bravo*, a German youth magazine, was published several consecutive years, becoming a household name. The same can be said of the 18 Herman collector's glasses commissioned by *Ritzenhoff*. In 2007, bids were made for 49 Herman paintings at a charity auction benefiting the Peter Maffay Foundation.

www.Kuenstler-Herman.de

**Want more? Here's an overview of all books
by Gianni, Jan & Marcello Liscia:**

Gianni, Jan & Marcello Liscia

D.R.E.A.M.
of
LEADERS

Leadership is not an Illusion

Illustrations:
Herman Reichold

ISBN: 978-3-744-88271-2 – 19,90 € (D), E-Book: 14,99 € (D)

Gianni, Jan & Marcello Liscia

WORKBOOK
RESPONSIBILITY

Showing responsibility for decisions made, for employees
and for oneself

Illustrations:
Herman Reichold

ISBN: 978-3-7528-5825-9 – 8,90 € (D), E-Book: 4,99 € (D)

Gianni, Jan & Marcello Liscia

WORKBOOK
EDUCATION

Personal and employee education

Illustrations:
Herman Reichold

ISBN: 978-3-7528-5826-6 – 8,90 € (D), E-Book: 4,99 € (D)

Gianni, Jan & Marcello Liscia

WORKBOOK
ATTITUDE

A question of personal attitude and values which are
lived and experienced

Illustrations:
Herman Reichold

ISBN: 978-3-7528-5827-3 – 8,90 € (D), E-Book: 4,99 € (D)

Gianni, Jan & Marcello Liscia

WORKBOOK
MOTIVATION

Being ready to perform is the basis for all action

Illustrations:
Herman Reichold

ISBN: 978-3-7528-5828-0 – 8,90 € (D), E-Book: 4,99 € (D)

Gianni, Jan & Marcello Liscia

The Book of Happiness

A work and reflection diary

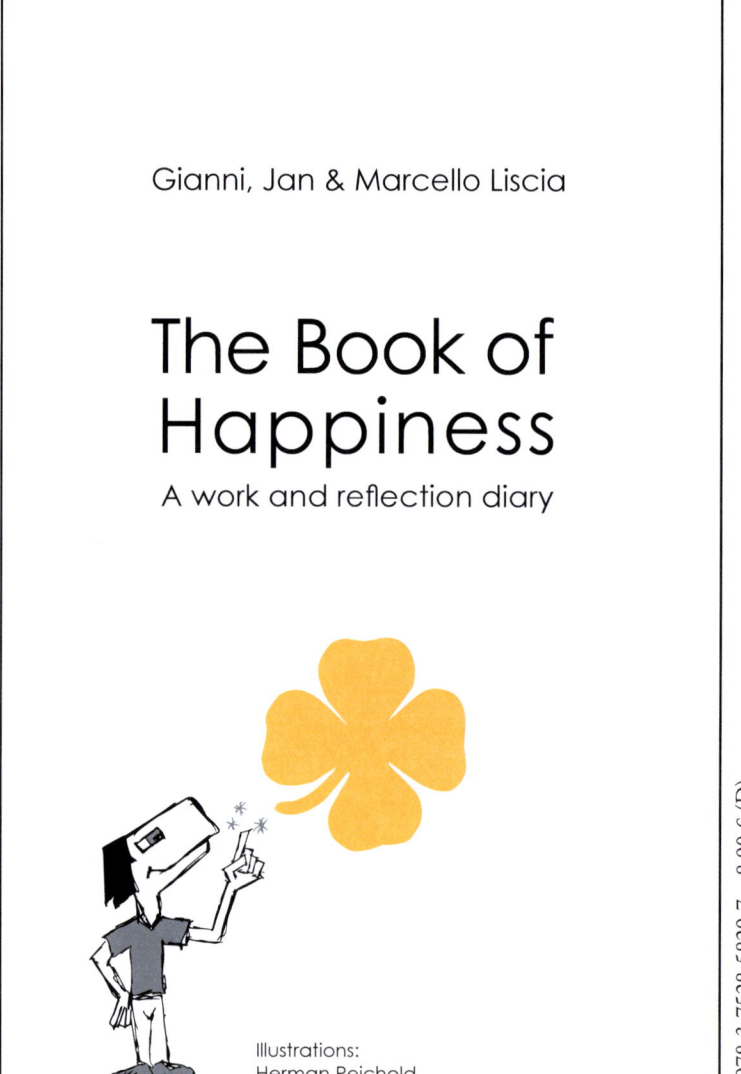

Illustrations:
Herman Reichold

ISBN: 9978-3-7528-5829-7 – 8,90 € (D)

All of our titles are available as ebooks (except The Book of Happiness) and can be enjoyed in the German language, too!